Strange Creatures

Strange creatures

Welcome to planet Earth...

In the modern world of satellites and communication networks,
there are still some animals that retain a prehistoric appearance,
or an aura of mystery. Horned devils, spiky dragons,
insects that look like leaves — our planet's creatures sometimes
appear to belong to the realm of science fiction
than the real world.

In this fantastic universe, living fortresses coexist
with electric fish, strange winged creatures look down
on lazy toothless beasts, while in the marine depths,
ghostly living lights illuminate the gloom.

These living things are strange in their behaviour,
or the way they have evolved, or simply in their appearance.

The colour of the glider's fur can range from cinnamon brown to pure black. This creature almost became an endangered species because its magnificent pelt was coveted by poachers. Fortunately, however, it proved impossible to tan correctly.

With built-in parachutes,
gliders
take to the air

A GLIDING MARSUPIAL

A strident call rings out in the forest-clad shores of eastern Australia; a small ball of fur has just leapt into the air. However, instead of falling, the seemingly suicidal animal stretches out its forelimbs and opens a broad 'parachute'. The greater glider, also called the greater flying phalanger or greater gliding possum, is a marsupial which can cover over 100 metres with each gliding flight; and, in six successive leaps, can volplane over half a kilometre. In company with flying squirrels, it is one of the few mammals that can travel through the air.

Gliders, like many marsupials, are fussy eaters: they feed exclusively on tender eucalyptus buds.

Profile

The greater glider
Schoinobates volans
Family: marsupial mammals
Size: around 50 cm (tail: almost 45 cm)
Weight: 1 kg to 1.5 kg
Habitat: thinly-populated eucalyptus forests in eastern Australia
Diet: eucalyptus buds
Predators: owls, foxes; also endangered by forest fires
Young: although female phalangers have 2 teats in their marsupial pouches, they rear only one young at a time, which stays in the pouch for 4 months

The greater glider uses a web of skin stretching from the middle of its forelimbs to its hind limbs as a parachute. Despite weighing more than 1 kilogram, the glider can cover around 100 metres in a single leap. The creature bends its forelimbs towards its jaw to achieve its characteristic delta-wing shape in flight.

With beaver-like tails, duck-like bills and webbed feet,
duck-billed platypuses
are unusual mammals, and ones that also lay eggs!

The winding passages of the platypus' burrow can reach a length of 18 metres and extend upwards into the bank for between 1 and 7 metres above the entrance, usually found near the water level. The female lines her nesting chamber with leaves brought back wrapped in her folded tail. This bedding is warm and wet enough to ensure that her eggs are well incubated. She will then only leave the burrow to forage for food.

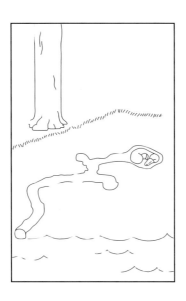

THE 'DUCKMOLE'

When, in 1797, surprised European naturalists first saw a stuffed duck-billed platypus or duckbill, they thought the animal had been assembled by colleagues as a hoax.

This small animal, nicknamed the 'duckmole' by the first Australian settlers, belongs to the order Monotremata, a small group of mammals that includes only three species: the duck-billed platypus and two echidnas (spiny anteaters) from the same region (Australia and New Guinea), which, like their reptilian ancestors, lay eggs and, like other mammals, suckle their young after birth; a difficult conundrum for zoologists.

The female platypus is oviparous or egg-laying: two weeks after mating, the female usually lays two soft-shelled, spherical eggs that are stuck together. This is clear proof that the platypus is related to the reptiles. Shortly after hatching, the hungry baby platypuses press up against their mother who, because she has no nipples, exudes the milk through slits in her abdomen.

The duck-billed platypus cannot survive long away from water. When it dives, its pelt traps a layer of air against its skin and this layer of 'insulating gas' enables it to brave extremely cold water. The species was threatened by extinction due to its practical pelt: during the 19th century, these animals were trapped for their fur.

With its cylindrical body, webbed feet and insulating pelt, the platypus is well adapted to diving in turbulent conditions and can stay up to five minutes under water. Unlike otters and beavers which swim using their hind limbs or by undulating their bodies, the duck-billed platypus uses its broad webbed forefeet to move through the water, reaching speeds of up to 3 to 4 kilometres an hour.

The duck-billed platypus, which is much smaller than commonly believed, rarely grows longer than 40 centimetres and does not weigh more than 2 kilograms. It spends most of its time in the water searching for food under stones or in the mud.

AN ELECTRIC 'BILL'...

Visibility is so poor in the murky water that the duck-billed platypus does not use its eyes to find its way around (it actually closes its eyes underwater) but its bill. This duck-like bill actually acts like a type of homing device: numerous electroreceptors enable the animal to detect changes in the electrical field produced by the movements of the insect larvae, worms or tadpoles

The burrow of the duck-billed platypus may have several openings, usually just above the water line. The passages leading to the nesting 'chamber' are just wide enough to accommodate the animal's body and they help to dry its pelt as it returns from the water. After the female has settled into her burrow to give birth, she blocks the burrow from the inside.

on which it feeds. Storing its prey in its cheek pouches, it resurfaces to float on its stomach and enjoy its meal at leisure.

...AND A POISONOUS SPUR

During the mating season, which lasts from August to October, the males use their spurs in fierce combat. These spurs, a centimetre long, are situated near the ankle of the hind limb and are connected to a venom-secreting gland in the upper part of the limb. The poison it produces, unique in mammals, is strong enough to kill a dog. If this small animal is irritated, it will not hesitate to attack a person's arms and hands. Its sting is intensely painful and causes a swelling which

The echidnas

The duck-billed platypus belongs to a very small family and its only two relations, the short-nosed and long-nosed echidnas or spiny anteaters from Australia and New Guinea, look nothing like it. However, like their cousin the duck-billed platypus, these primitive mammals do lay eggs. The spiny anteaters resemble hedgehogs rather than ducks, and their long narrow snout enables them to root out ants and termites.

spreads rapidly to the rest of the limb. This inflammation may last several days and being stung in this way can cause drowsiness in some cases. In view of all these things, it is probably advisable to give this peculiar-looking animal a wide berth!

The echidnas, the only relations of the duck-billed platypus, are covered in spines like those of hedgehogs. Their webbed feet are equipped with strong claws which they use to remove unwanted parasites. But the strangest thing about these small animals is their life expectancy: they can live to the ripe old age of 49.

Colourful and outlandish,
chameleons
are born with a baleful glare

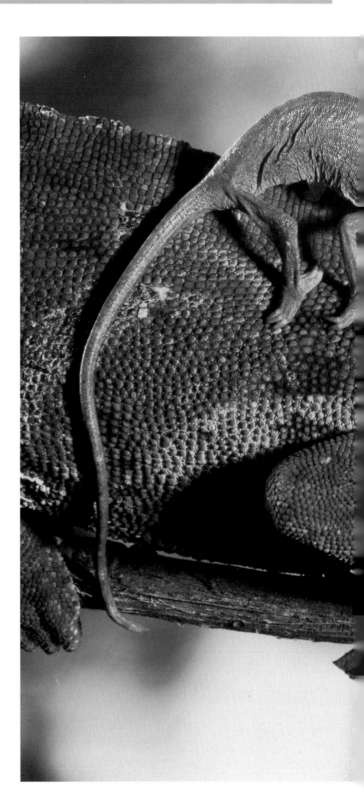

TELESCOPIC EYES

Chameleons are not likely to get a crick in their neck as they never need to look over their shoulder. They can look at the sky and the ground at the same time because each of their eyes swivels independently. The chameleon's visual field covers 180 degrees – comparable to that of a 100–135 millimetre telephoto lens.

THE COLOURS OF EMOTION

The chameleon is reputed to change its colour like a shirt and this ability has been attributed to its need to blend in with its surroundings. But if it senses danger, the chameleon may turn red with anxiety or pale with anger, while a frightened chameleon may display brown and yellow stripes on its skin. This would be a strange way indeed of trying to pass unnoticed but, in actual fact, as most of its enemies cannot detect colours, it does not matter.

Profile

European chameleon
Chamaeleo chamaeleon
Family: Chamaeleonidae
Size: 20 cm to 48 cm

Habitat: dunes, coastal forests, desert areas, shrubby savannahs in Africa, Asia and Europe.
Diet: insects
Young: oval eggs hatch after 6 to 9 months depending on the temperature
Life expectancy: several years
Social structure: chameleons are solitary animals

Many legends have been inspired by the chameleon's outlandish appearance. In Madagascar, where chameleons are plentiful, it is believed that this creature can cause blindness with a flick of its tongue. According to a Malagasy proverb, fate is like a chameleon: sometimes you only have to whistle for it to change colour.

This touching scene is short-lived. After hatching, young chameleons only remain on their mother's back for a short time before starting to lead the solitary life of an adult. After the first few weeks, the young chameleon, no larger than 4 centimetres, goes off in search of insects that are often too big for its mouth.

Brightly-coloured chameleons bask in the sun...

The chameleon uses its jagged, irregular outline to camouflage itself. In addition to this, its body constantly rocks, as if unsteady, and, in vegetation ruffled by the breeze, this trembling movement helps to conceal it.

A SWIFT AND ACCURATE TONGUE

Chameleons use their incredibly fast tongue to hunt: it shoots out in a fraction of a second, catching insects at a distance of anything up to 20 centimetres. A chameleon can therefore catch around four flies on the wing in the space of three seconds! It then conveys its victims back to its mouth by retracting its tongue. But the insatiable chameleon is no fool: it takes care to swallow wasps and bees quickly before they can sting it.

With its three frontal horns, Jackson's chameleon looks like a miniature triceratops. But only the male wears this ornamental helmet; the female has only one, much smaller, horn. Surprisingly for reptiles, chameleons are viviparous, in other words, the females give birth to live young.

Although the various species differ greatly, chameleons form a homogenous group. They all have a flattened body, a high, narrow cranium, pincer-like feet, independently movable eyes and a long, extensile tongue. With the exception of several desert species, most chameleons are tree-dwellers.

Chameleons are renowned for their ability to change colour, but this ability is not as extensive as is commonly believed. In fact, each species has only one possible pattern of colour changes. For example, the panther chameleon has dark-red cross bands and a green horizontal stripe. But if it catches sight of itself in the mirror, it turns very pale.

This living fossil moves around like a military tank.

Horseshoe crabs
brave wind and tides

AN ARMOUR-PLATED SUBMARINE

Although these shells circling on the ocean beds may look like giant crabs, turtles or submarines, they are in fact giant scorpions; or rather one of their ancestors, the horseshoe crab. In fact, this fortress of the deep is the oldest living representative of the Chelicerate family, the branch that gave birth to spiders and scorpions. Like the latter, horseshoe crabs have, in the place of antennae, a small pair of pincers (chelicerae) and, at the rear of the body, a tail-spine which, in the case of these sea tanks, is not poisonous. These huge creatures which can grow as large as 60 centimetres, including the tail-spine, are completely harmless.

This soldier's helmet is actually a horseshoe crab. Two large compound eyes, like those of insects, are situated on each side of its shell. But the creature can also see behind through a row of smaller simple 'eyes' (ocelli) on top of its shell.

The two movable plates covering the animal's back conceal four pairs of jointed legs and various appendages. The horseshoe crab pushes its horseshoe-shaped shell in front of it to dig into the seabed or to make its escape. It uses its pincers to catch all types of small marine animals and convey them to its mouth, strangely situated on the side, between the top part of its legs.

Horseshoe crabs are particularly at home on the muddy, sandy seabeds of South East Asia and the east coast of North America. In the spawning season, they migrate in droves to shallower waters to reproduce, which results in massive numbers of these creatures together in one place.

Sloths are the most common mammals in the South American tropical rainforests. They occur in equatorial rainforests, semi-arid tropical forests and even in gardens. Excellent swimmers, sloths have been spotted crossing the Panama Canal to take up residence on Barro Colorado island. Once a week, sloths descend to the ground to defecate in a small hole hollowed out with their embryonic tail.

Leisurely creatures, **sloths** live life upside down

AN INCREDIBLE ANIMAL

The aptly-named sloth spends 14 hours out of 24 resting. At the top of its form, it covers only 38 metres per day and spends most of its time in the trees, feeding on leaves, its only food. The sloth is the only quadruped that lives hanging upside down and, in company with armadillos and anteaters, is one of the oldest mammals in the world, having appeared 60 million years ago. The only sloths to have survived to this day are very small (no longer than 60 centimetres) and very shy. The round face of certain species displays a fixed, charming smile. Their extremely mobile heads can swivel through 90 degrees because their necks possess nine cervical vertebrae (other mammals only have seven).

The long claws of the sloth are particularly well adapted to clinging to branches. Mainly tree-dwellers, sloths eat non-stop, probably to compensate for the poor nutritional value of the leaves that form their exclusive diet. Their extremely slow digestive systems resemble those of ruminants: sloths' intestines have several compartments which break down the cellulose.

The striking orange mark, called the speculum, on the back of some sloths corresponds to a glandular area whose function is still a mystery. Despite the countless insects living in their pelt, sloths have no fleas.

A sloth's hair grows in the opposite direction to that of other animals, from belly to back, and is rarely groomed. This negligence combined with the grooved structure of the individual hairs allows the growth of a single-celled alga, as well as providing a home for around 120 butterflies and 1000 species of Coleoptera. As a result, the sloth's pelt takes on a greenish tint which gives protective camouflage.

Like aliens from another planet
bioluminescent creatures
light up the gloom with their strange glow

A LOST WORLD

It was long thought that the ocean depths were like a desert devoid of any type of life, but nothing could be further from the truth. Even in the deepest trenches, 11,000 metres below the surface, a strange fauna moves through the dark. These animals are able to distinguish friends from foes in this unfathomable gloom by means of a built-in flashlight: they emit their own bioluminescent light.

BIOLUMINESCENCE: A MAGICAL LIGHT

These animals have organs called photophores which specialize in the production of light. They all contain molecules, such as luciferin, which, as a result of a complex chemical reaction, emit a phosphorescent light. Often these animals do not make the luciferin themselves. Symbiotic bacteria, living in their photophores, produce the bioluminescence for them. This 'artificial' lighting

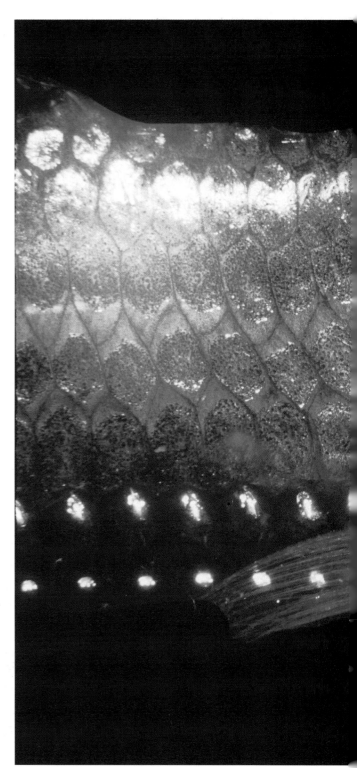

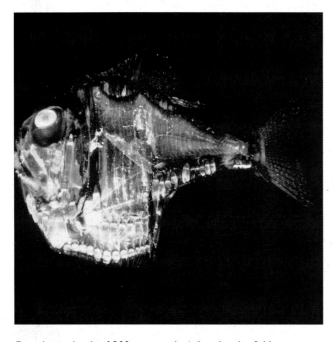

Found at a depth of 300 metres, the 'silver hatchetfish' owes its name to its distinctive shape, metallic colour and telescopic eyes directed upward. It has many bioluminescent organs along its stomach.

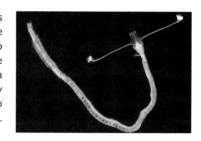

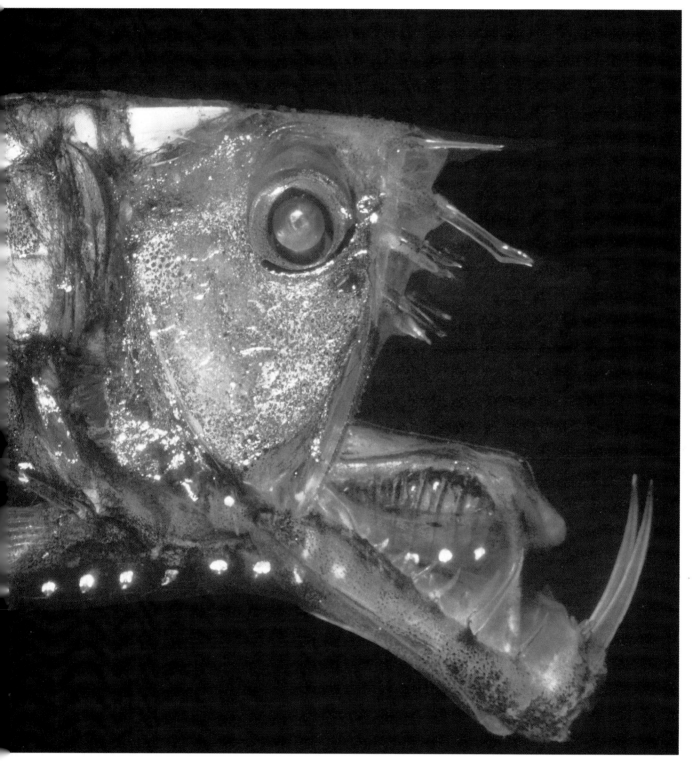

With its bioluminescent organs, this 25-centimetre monster can be seen from afar. The long teeth of the *chauliodus* or deep-sea viperfish are reminiscent of the fangs of poisonous snakes. These fish are just as at home in arctic or tropical oceans. During the day, they lurk at a depth of 1800 metres, but at night they come up to 450 metres.

The deep-sea anglerfish uses its luminous antenna as a fishing rod. It waves this bright organ in front of its mouth to attract prey in the gloom. Victims sometimes even larger than the deep-sea anglerfish fall into the trap.

Descent to the depths

Exploring the ocean depths is still extremely dangerous. The light gradually fades as the water gets deeper, disappearing completely at a depth of 500 metres. At 1000 metres the water exerts a pressure of 100 kilograms on every centimetre of skin and the temperature is close to 0ºC throughout the year. No other region is so hostile to life. However, scientists can now reach the bottom with the aid of bathyscaphes, pocket submarines and other special diving aids that provide protection from the terrible pressure, which can reduce even the hardiest animal to a pulp.

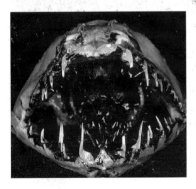

Deep-sea fish have an insatiable appetite. *Chauliodus* or deep-sea viperfish attack prey so much larger than themselves that it seems hard to believe they can swallow them. In fact, their cervical vertebrae swivel enabling them to open their mouths very wide.

always forms a precise pattern on the animal's body, creating a distinctive luminous signature: extremely practical for identifying potential partners. But some, like the deep-sea anglerfish, use this light to hunt: it lures prey towards their gaping mouth.

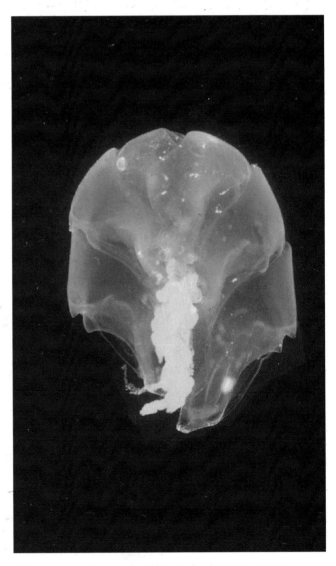

When touched, the jellyfish, *Hippopodius hippopus*, emits a surprising light. This soft, luminous creature is only a few centimetres long.

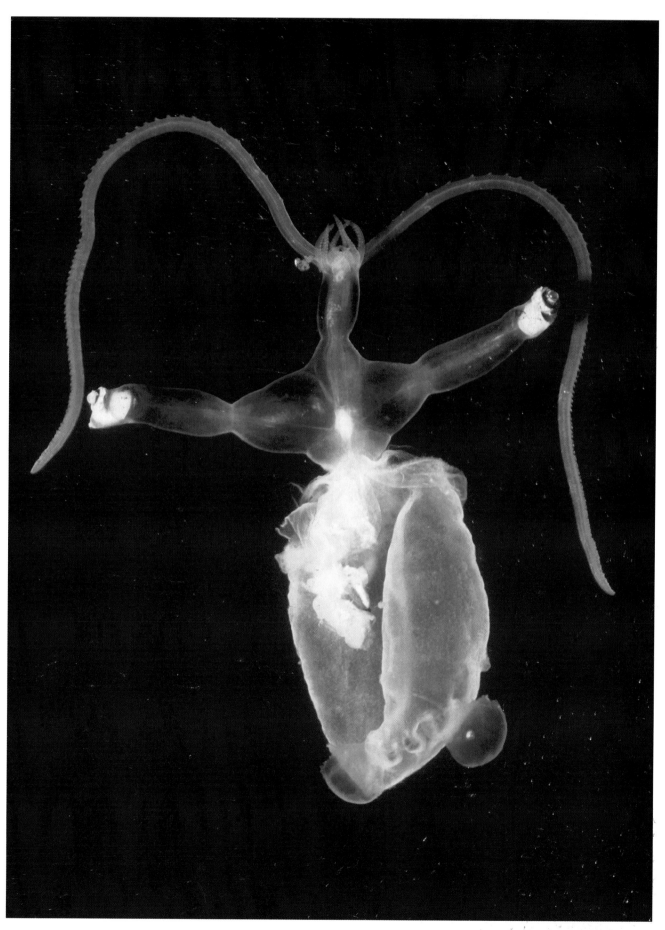

Many cephalopods (octopus family) inhabit the ocean deeps. This *bathothauma*, a small, deep-sea squid, is uniquely adapted to life under pressure and in the dark. A mournful light shines through its transparent body. Its telescopic eyes, fixed at the end of two movable stalks, enable the *bathothauma* to survey the depths.

Although this luminous garland looks as if it should belong draped over a Christmas tree, it lives 3000 metres under the sea. Besides a double row of light organs running along its needle-shaped body, this stomiatoid has a barbel tipped with a powerful photophore. Like many deep-sea fish, stomiatoids have gargantuan mouths.

American fireflies (glow-worms) flashing their lights after nightfall.

NATURAL NIGHT LIGHTS

The phenomenon of bioluminescence is not restricted to deep-sea creatures: many glow-worms and other fireflies on dry land flash signals to attract the opposite sex at nightfall. This ability manifests itself early: even the larvae are luminescent, although they use these flash patterns to warn potential predators about the bitter taste of their flesh and not to participate in elaborate courting rituals.

American fireflies attract females by dazzling them. The male produces a regular pattern of flashes and the willing female replies after a set time characteristic of the species. When large groups of these insects gather together, they flash more or less in unison, so that the tree in which they have congregated flashes on and off in time to their signals.

At the reptilian masked ball
frilled lizards
are among the best-dressed

The frilled lizard is probably the most famous lizard in Australia. It ranges mainly through the north and north-east of this continent, but is also found in Papua New Guinea. This reptile lives mainly in the trees where it feeds on insects, spiders and small rodents. Its size is rather surprising: from tail to snout, it measures about a metre.

AN AGGRESSIVE DRAGON

'Appearances can be deceptive' would be the perfect motto for the frilled lizard, an Australian reptile which, at first glance, might pass unnoticed. But this small creature has the unfortunate habit of changing into a dragon at the slightest provocation. If disturbed by a fierce enemy or a forward female, the frilled lizard fans out its impressive neck frill, spitting and hissing as if it were the most terrifying creature on Earth. This performance, which zoologists call a 'threat display', is actually all bluff. It is a protective device employed by many animals to make them seem bigger and more dangerous than they really are.

Let sleeping dragons lie! When irritated or mating, the frilled lizard suddenly erects its coloured neck membrane and presents a very different image. This is actually a threat display: this insectivorous lizard would not hurt a fly unless, of course, it were hungry.

A FOLD-AWAY FRILL

The scaly frill of this strange reptile usually lies folded over its shoulders. It is supported by a row of cartilaginous rods and is often brightly coloured with black, white, brown, bright pink and yellow spots. When the animal begins its threat display or when mating, it opens its mouth wide, causing the frill to extend in all its glory. This fold of skin can reach a diameter of 30 centimetres in adult males and, to appear even more intimidating, frilled lizards rise up on their two hind legs.

They then produce a characteristic hissing sound and whip the ground in a threatening manner with their tail. This vertical posture has another

advantage: it also allows the lizard to prepare for a quick escape because, although it may pretend to be a dragon, it is not naturally aggressive and will run away if its display does not have the desired effect.

Despite its frightening appearance, the frilled lizard is a coward. If its threat display does not work, it takes to its heels, running on its two hind legs with its forelegs in the air and using its tail for balance. Like the basilisk, it is a champion sprinter.

With their extraordinarily long noses,
nut weevils
are no natural beauties

Despite its comical, even quaint, appearance, the nut weevil causes a great deal of damage. Although the weevil's larvae only mature in nuts, the adults also attack pears, peaches and, occasionally, apples, plums and cherries. As a result, this insect, less than 8 millimetres long, is the bane of fruit farmers and orchard owners.

A LONG-NOSED SCOURGE

Curculio nucum is the scientific name given to the nut weevil. Although it looks slightly ridiculous, this strange insect, particularly the female, wields a keen blade capable of piercing the hardest nut. The female nut weevil's rostrum or snout, longer than that of the male, enables her to drill a hole in nuts in which she lays 25 to 30 eggs. When they hatch, the larvae eat their way into the heart of the fruit and live there for two months, feeding on the raw kernel. Wormy and inedible, the infected nuts fall from the tree early.

The nut weevil mainly attacks the fruit of the tree it parasitizes. But it also likes the leaves of the nut tree, which it carefully pierces with its long, curved snout. Leaves in the shade are the worst affected, because the nut weevil likes cool places.
Once its leaves are patterned with a tracery of holes, the tree loses valuable strength and is at risk.

This female is laying her eggs in a nut. When the larva emerges from the fruit, it falls to the ground and spins a cocoon between the roots of the nut tree. The larva pupates for one to three years, metamorphosing into an adult once the harsh winter has passed.

A cross between a hare and a pig
aardvarks
are cowardly creatures

A frightened gaze, soft rabbit's ears and the snout of a suckling pig; for many predators, the aardvark or African ant bear, similar to a 100-kilogram hare, is a tasty morsel. The aardvark has only one means of protecting itself: it rolls on to its back and strikes out at predators with its powerful claws. However, rapid flight to the safety of its burrow is a much more effective line of defence.

THE 'EARTH-PIG'

At night, the African savannah comes alive: many timorous, non-aggressive animals, the prey of wild beasts during the day, make the most of the coolness of the night to go about their business. In the torch light, what looks like a giant hare, almost 2 metres long, scurries off. Despite its hurried escape, the animal turns round, revealing a glimpse of its curiously-shaped head: the runaway has cone-shaped ears and a tapering muzzle ending in a pig's snout. This chimera is called an aardvark or an African ant bear. After shooting a last dejected glance at its assailants, the creature disappears down into a hole.

During the day, the aardvark stays in its comfortable burrow. Its strong claws enable it to dig up to 2 metres of passages through the hardest soil. The burrows are located near termite nests, the aardvark's favourite food. To avoid intrusion by uninvited guests, such as pythons, jackals or hyenas, the 'earth-pig' blocks the entrance to its home.

The aardvark lives mainly in the savannahs to the south of the Sahara. It is also found in the virgin forests of Cameroon and the Congo. Two million years ago, aardvarks ranged as far as Southern Europe. Aardvarks prefer to live in regions where termites are plentiful. They also seem to be fond of a particular species of the gourd family (Cucurbitaceae), called the 'aardvark pumpkin' because it is found in the vicinity of their burrows.

A HYBRID NOCTURNAL ANIMAL

The aardvark clearly owes its nickname 'earth-pig' to its pig-like snout and deep burrow. This hybrid animal displays the characteristics of such different creatures that it was very difficult to find a place for it in the scientific classification of animals. It was long believed to be a distant relative of the anteater because of its insect-based diet. But no true relationship has been found to exist between these two creatures.

This orphan's family connections are revealed by the way it walks: whether moving forward or backward, the aardvark places all its weight on its toes. It has therefore been placed in the order Ungulata, with horses: the aardvark is full of surprises. It is also virtually impossible to catch a glimpse of this animal in its natural habitat, the African savannah. It spends the day sleeping in its burrow and only comes out in complete darkness to seek out its favourite food, termites, which it catches with its sticky tongue.

The aardvark is a very shy animal: once night has fallen, it emerges tentatively from its burrow. It stays nearby for several minutes to make sure there are no enemies about, then trots away in search of food, stopping often and swivelling its telescopic ears to listen for the possible presence of a predator.

DIY experts of the sea,
hammerhead sharks, sawfish and American paddlefish
own their own tools

Hammerhead sharks usually keep to the open seas. They frequent the warm waters of the Atlantic, the Indian Ocean and the Pacific. They have also been spotted near the coast of the West Indies, California and even in the Mediterranean. Hammerhead sharks are huge creatures which can grow to a length of 5 metres or more. The purpose of their strangely-shaped heads is still a mystery.

A USEFUL TOOLBOX

Some cartilaginous fish, such as sharks and rays, resemble exhibits at a DIY exhibition. Ideal for odd jobs around the home, the hammerhead shark has a T-shaped head. Its eyes, as well as its nostrils, are situated at either end of the lobes of the 'hammer'. The large distance between its eyes prevents the shark from looking straight ahead and, as a result, it swims circling from left to right.

The sawfish, which belongs to the ray family, would be the ideal helpmate for a carpenter. Its elongated snout is edged with long sharp teeth.

When it nears the coast, the hammerhead shark behaves like a rubbish truck, swallowing everything within reach, including cans and old plastic containers. It usually feeds on fish and cuttlefish but, when food is short, it can represent a danger to bathers.

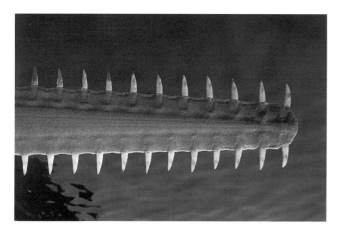

The sawfish is particularly well equipped.

KITCHEN UTENSILS AND HOME DECORATION

The task of refurnishing follows any major structural work. The carpet shark deserves to be given pride of place in the living room. Delicate fringes or barbels edge its magnificently-patterned beige and off-white body. Cartilaginous fish also offer a range of kitchen utensils. The American paddlefish, for example, has a long, flat spoon-shaped snout which it uses to detect food and guide organisms towards its mouth.

The carpet shark prefers to camouflage itself to attack its prey. The numerous barbels (fringes) which hang from its body resemble algae and the cunning creature hides in forests of rockweed (fucus) or in rocky areas. Carpet sharks live in shallow, tropical waters, particularly near the Australian coast.

With its flat, elongated snout, the American paddlefish can grow to a length of 1.8 metres. This cartilaginous fish lives exclusively in fresh water, preferably in the large sandy-bottomed rivers and lakes of North America. It prefers calm water, rich in the animal and plant plankton on which it feeds.

Due to pollution, dams and excessive fishing, the American paddlefish is now in grave danger of extinction. At the turn of the century, American paddlefish fishing was a booming industry: in the United States, close on 1000 tonnes per year were caught. It was popular for its flesh and its roe, similar to that of the sturgeon.

The single egg laid by the female armadillo systematically subdivides into four so that four genetically-identical baby armadillos are born: four natural clones.

Like antediluvian tanks,
armadillos
are safe from predators

A FORTIFIED SHELL

With its scarab-like armour, its rabbit-like ears and its elongated head tapering to a small snout, the armadillo is in a class of its own. In company with the sloth and the anteaters, which are also exclusive to America, it belongs to one of the oldest families of mammals: Edentata.

When afraid, the armadillo flattens itself against the ground, making it difficult for would-be predators to get a purchase. Some armadillos, like the hairy armadillo or the three-banded armadillo, are able to roll themselves into a tight ball. On their feet, the spur-shaped scales make it possible to 'lock and bar' the fortress. The nine-banded armadillo will

Profile

Armadillo
Dasypus
Family: toothless mammals (Edentata)
Size: from 24 cm to 57 cm (over 1 m in the case of the giant armadillo)
Weight: 4 kg to 6 kg (giant armadillo 60 kg)
Habitat: North and South America; avoids arid and icy areas
Diet: insectivore with omnivorous tendencies
Predators: lynx, puma, bear
Life expectancy: between 12 and 15 years

The bony scales covering the armadillo's skin are joined in plates or bands around its body and in rings around its tail. When the armadillo curls up, even a jaguar finds it difficult to crack open this armour-plated ball.

Particularly well adapted to digging, the armadillo's powerful, stocky limbs have sharp claws, which the animal uses to dig its burrow.

sometimes leap into the air to frighten its attacker. Unfortunately, when in front of a car, this brings the animal level with the bumper and it is killed outright.

THE TEXAN MASCOT

The 'tortoise-rabbit', as it was called by the ancient Aztecs, became very popular in the middle of the last century. In Mexico, people craved its flesh as well as its company. In Florida, a pair of captive armadillos, having escaped in the 1920s, populated the entire peninsula. Since 1980, this small animal has been the official emblem of Texas, where they often hold armadillo races, as well as armadillo barbecues. The armadillo is fairly hardy. It lives both in tropical forests and in the South American savannahs; in the mountains it can climb as high as 3000 metres. But, unlike many other animals, the armadillo does not mark its territory and, outside the mating season, remains completely solitary.

The burrow of the armadillo can measure between 1 and 7 metres long and around 20 centimetres in diameter. The wider nesting area is at the far end of this passage and the armadillo backs in. It carries in leaves and grass to make it more comfortable. In the summer, the animal only comes out of its burrow at night, but if the temperature is cool, it takes advantage of the midday sun to hunt.

Who's afraid of the
death's head hawk moth
a simple honey-eater?

With its macabre mask, the death's head hawk moth *(Acherontia atropos)* has, since Antiquity, had a funereal reputation. Its latin name is derived from 'Acheron', the mythological river that flowed to the underworld. In fact only its caterpillar is poisonous.

AN IMPERSONATOR MOTH

The death's head moth has macabre markings 'tattooed' on its thorax. This skull-like pattern is regarded as an evil omen and has earned this harmless moth the same type of unsavoury reputation as the black cat. The death's head moth feeds in a very unusual way. Although other hawk moths have a long, slender proboscis, the death's head moth has a short, stiff proboscis which it uses, at night, to bore into beehives and drink the honey. To avoid being caught, this cunning thief imitates the sound made by the bees, producing a chirping noise by sucking air into its head. Like the spells chanted by a witch doctor, the hypnotic song of the death's head moth pacifies the worker bees.

Hawk moths, also known as sphinx moths, have a full wing span of over 10 centimetres and are very hard to miss. These moths are excellent fliers: by beating their wings extremely fast, they can hover above the flowers to gather nectar. They also play an important role in the pollination of a large number of plants.

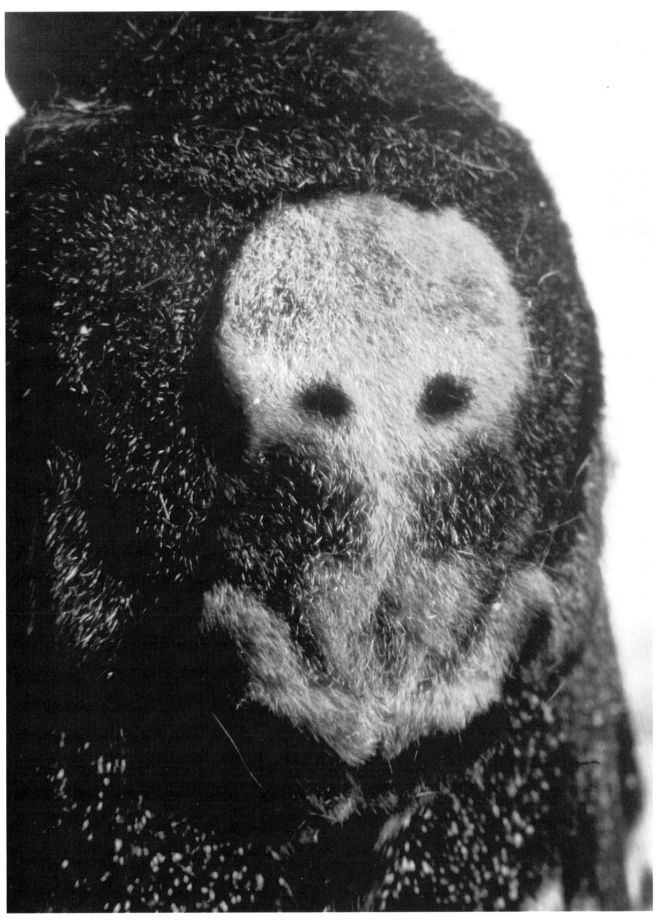

Every day is Halloween for the death's head moth. But despite its sinister appearance, it does not sting or bite and is not poisonous.
However, the hawk moth caterpillar is best avoided because it feeds mainly on a poisonous plant, belladonna, and becomes toxic in its turn.
It can safely go about its business in full view, as birds steer well clear of it.

Puffed-up
porcupine fish
show off their lethal spines

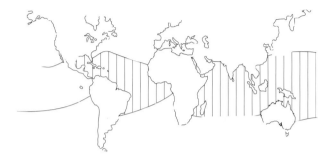

Porcupine fish of the genus Diodon are mainly found in warm tropical waters. They occur in salt water but never in fresh water. Poor swimmers, porcupine fish cannot swim against the current and it is not unusual for some of them to be washed up on the beaches of Europe. They are even found fairly frequently on the shores of the Mediterranean.

A PORCUPINE FISH

The placid porcupine fish uses water to good effect. When threatened, or disturbed, this brightly-coloured fish, which usually blends in with the coral reefs in tropical seas, inflates its body by drawing in water and erects its needle-sharp spines. Few predators would be foolish enough to swallow a spiny ball of lethal bristles.

Passive resistance is virtually its only line of defence. Escape is not really an option, as the porcupine fish cannot get far with its diminutive fins. Being as manoeuvrable as a pocket submarine, the porcupine fish has to rely on its skills as a quick-change artist. At the slightest hint of danger,

When safe from danger, the needle-like scales of the porcupine fish lay flat against its body. This strange fish inhabits coral reefs, which are also frequented by sharks and other predators. With its small fins, the porcupine fish cannot make a quick escape, so its only line of defence is to blow up its body and erect its spines.

the porcupine fish swallows a large quantity of salt water that directly fills its stomach and inflates it like a balloon.

...THAT TURNS INTO A BALLOON AND SPITS AT ITS FOOD

Without ribs and pelvis, the porcupine fish can swell to two or three times its normal size, and even its spine can bend. Its spiny scales are erected and the animal becomes as appetizing as a prickly chestnut.

Porcupine fish have a beak-like mouth lined with fused teeth which forms a natural bottle-opener used to open and crush shellfish. To locate these molluscs, porcupine fish eject water at the sand in order to expose their prey. Even when living in an aquarium, porcupine fish continue to spit water at their prey: they project a stream of water at the hand that has just fed them.

Puffers: deadly despite their lack of spines

Like the porcupine fish, the puffer or globefish (tetraodon) swells up with water but has no spines. When washed up on the shore, puffers blow up with air and children often use them as balls. But extreme care must be taken if they are featured on the menu: these fish contain an extremely virulent poison: tetraodontoxin. Only a specially-trained cook can safely prepare 'fugu', a popular Japanese speciality.

When irritated, the porcupine fish swallows a great deal of water and balloons like a water skin, swelling to an impressive size and erecting its spines. Even the hungriest shark would hesitate to attack this spiny ball, especially as some species measure more than a metre long.

Brightly-coloured, hairy, misshapen or outlandish,
primates
are our distant relatives

Goeldie's marmoset is a small extremely rare monkey from South America. It bears a passing resemblance to a Yorkshire terrier, has little rounded ears and an unusual muzzle. The darling of zoologists, it was named *callimico*, which means 'beautiful little monkey' in Latin. There is still some controversy about its place in the zoological classification, since it displays characteristics common to several families of primates.

SMALL MONKEY, GIANT FINGER

The order of primates is often taken to refer to chimpanzees and gorillas; but monkeys are not all almost human in appearance. Lemurs, probably the most primitive of the primates, win the prize for originality. The mouse lemurs from Madagascar look like scale models. Their tiny heads have two large ears and a pair of wide-open eyes well adapted to nocturnal life.

The harmless aye-aye lives in the same Malagasy forests and numerous legends have sprung up around its weird appearance: anyone killing an aye-aye is doomed to die within the year. This is why the people of Madagascar have never harmed

Mouse lemurs live in the rainforests and bamboo thickets of Madagascar. They rarely grow larger than the human thumb and weigh around 50 grams. The cry of mouse lemurs is so shrill that it is barely detectable by the human ear and may even be confused with sounds made by insects. Mouse lemurs feed mainly on grasshoppers and beetles.

A cross between a rat and a monkey, the aye-aye might have inspired the makers of Gremlins. The strangest part of the anatomy of this 50-centimetre long Malagasy primate, is its extremely long middle finger which it uses to search for food. It taps the branches with this finger to detect hollows that may contain the insect larvae on which it feeds.

The mandrills live in the dense tropical rainforests of Africa. Most of the time, they remain on the ground searching for food: roots, fruit, insects and snakes. At night, they climb into the trees to sleep.

Profile

Mandrill
mandrillus sphinx
Family: mammalian primate
Size: 80 cm

Weight: 50 kg
Habitat: rainforests of central Africa
Diet: omnivorous
Young: the female usually has only one young at a time; she tends its carefully for several months
Life expectancy: around 30 years
Predators: snakes, humans

the aye-aye. However, these creatures are now so rare that they have become an extremely endangered species.

DONNING THE MASK

Mouse lemurs and aye-ayes may avoid drawing attention to themselves, but the colourful mandrill is no shrinking violet. The dominant male of this species of large monkey wears a vividly-coloured 'mask', immediately recognizable to members of the same species. The more excited the mandrill grows, the brighter its colours become. Similarly, in the case of the proboscis monkeys of Borneo, only the males have large noses. With age, these noses gradually increase in size until they droop down over their mouth so, when they want to eat, elderly proboscis monkeys have to push their cucumber-shaped nose to one side. The function of such a monstrous organ remains a mystery but it may serve as a voice amplifier for the loud, drawn-out calls made by the males.

The parti-coloured face of the mandrill, as well as its chest, wrists, ankles, buttocks and penis play a specific role in communicating with other members of the group.

This unattractive, yet rather quaint face belongs to the proboscis monkey. Only adult males have this huge nose: females and young proboscis monkeys have small attractive upturned noses. The proboscis monkey is also an excellent swimmer and diver: it can stay under the water for almost half a minute, so its nose may function as a type of snorkel.

In the dense forests of Borneo, a loud 'honk' similar to the sound of a horn is heard: this is the proboscis monkey using his cucumber-shaped nose to amplify his mating call. Proboscis monkeys live in the swamps and on riverbanks, where they feed mainly on buds and young leaves.

This proboscis monkey could have been a model for the French sculptor, Rodin's The Thinker. Proboscis monkeys are very sociable and always move around in large numbers. They are also extremely docile animals and, in their country of origin, are still raised as pets.

Animals that refuses to grow old:
axolotls
will not turn into salamanders

The axolotl is a type of salamander that can measure up to 30 centimetres long. Its natural habitat is very restricted: in the wild it is only found in Lake Xochimilco, 20 kilometres south of Mexico. It is far more common in biological laboratories where scientists study its development and the functioning of the glands responsible for retarding its growth.

A TADPOLE ALL ITS LIFE

For frogs, tritons and other batrachians, the transformation from youth to maturity is fundamental. This is the rite of passage that turns the young tadpole wriggling through the water into a big toad leaping through the woodland. However, some batrachians, like the axolotl, refuse to grow old, retaining their immature appearance and their youthful features: gills and skin still suited to living in the water alongside teeth and eyelids and the tail of a tadpole. Despite its underdeveloped appearance the axolotl does manage to reproduce. This extraordinary phenomenon of apparent agelessness is called neoteny.

This Axolotl albinos categorically refuses to undergo the metamorphosis which will turn it into an adult. It retains its large red tufted gills, its tail, its aquatic skin and appearance… just like a tadpole. Nonetheless it is sexually mature and despite its pre-pubescent appearance it is able to produce numerous and healthy offspring. The axolotl can live as long as 25 years in this state.

A SURPRISING DISCOVERY

When the axolotl was discovered in the Mexican forests in the 18th century, scientists thought that this animal could metamorphose from one moment to the next and they did not know what to call it. However, in 1864 the Museum of Natural History in Paris, France, received six living axolotls: when one of the females laid a clutch of eggs, a number of the offspring – to general surprise and for no apparent reason – metamorphosed into a familiar species of salamander, the *Ambystoma Mexicanum*. This demonstrated that the axolotl and the ambystoma are in fact two forms of the same animal. The key to the difference is the thyroid gland: in the axolotl it

functions poorly and does not supply enough iodine. Indeed, in water which contains sufficient iodine the axolotl becomes a fully formed land-dwelling adult within a few weeks, while in water with a low iodine content it retains its immature appearance. Thus the mystery of the axolotl was solved – yet the creature retains its fearsome name, which means 'aquatic monster' in the Aztec language.

Just give an axolotl and iodine-rich bath and it will metamorphose into an ambystoma. The two are in fact the same animal, but the ambystoma lives on land: it has lost its gills, its skin is tougher and its tail no longer has any fins. This metamorphosis has never been observed in the wild: it has only been seen in laboratory conditions.

Scaly and prehistoric-looking,
pangolins
make good use of their tails

HALF ANIMAL, HALF PINE CONE

The pangolin is one of nature's curiosities: its body is covered with large scales which fit together like those of a fish, giving it a distinctly prehistoric appearance. Like anteaters, pangolins have extended tongues (up to 40 centimetres long in the larger species) with a sticky surface enabling them to catch insects and termites, their favourite food. Except for the giant pangolin, most of the species are tree-dwellers. Thanks to their powerful claws these scaly creatures can climb trees with astonishing agility. Just hold a pangolin upside down and you will see the proof: it will even attempt to climb up its own tail. They climb up trees with a caterpillar-like movement. Pangolins' tails are essential to them. The tail of the long-tailed pangolin, which can measure up to twice as long as the rest of its body, holds the record for the number of vertebrae in a mammal: 47. It also serves another purpose: young pangolins can ride horseback on their mother's tail.

Profile

Giant pangolin
Manis gigantea
Family: Pholidota
Size: 80 cm
Weight: 5 kg

Habitat: the giant pangolin lives in the rainforests and the tropical regions of Africa. Other species live in India, Sri Lanka, Malaysia and throughout the Indonesian peninsula.
Diet: ants and termites only
Young: all the young are the same size, around 25 cm, whatever the species.

Pangolins can roll themselves into a ball, wrapping their tail around their body, as a way of deterring most predators. Even humans can find it difficult to unroll the largest species of pangolin. If all else fails the animal has another unexpected defence strategy: it sprays its attacker with urine.

This may look like a scene from *Jurassic Park*; in fact it is a dense tropical forest in India. The giant pangolin looks calm and casual enough in a moment of safety. Yet these animals can also move extremely fast. Some can run at more than 3.6 kilometres per hour, holding themselves upright and using their tails for balance in the same way that kangaroos do.

51

Soft, irregular or spiky shells:
tortoises
have some surprising disguises

Soft-shelled tortoises are only found in fresh water. The unusual nose of this *Trionyx certilsfiomis* has a small snout at the end with which the tortoise forages in the mud.

SOFT, BUT DEFINITELY NOT STUPID!

Among the 260 tortoise species recorded worldwide, some exhibit unusual forms of disguise, quite different from the traditional image of the hard-shelled tortoise ambling gently through the garden.

Soft-shelled tortoises do not have a shell at all: instead of horny scales they have a thick skin with a leather-like consistency. In newly-hatched tortoises this skin has some hard patches, but these soon disappear. Because their protective covering is weaker, most of these soft-shelled tortoises (which are carnivores) are extraordinarily mobile and quick to bite.

The matamata is undoubtedly the strangest tortoise of all. Its flat triangular head ends in a soft snout and its body is covered with fleshy protuberances which have a seaweed-like appearance. In aquaria the matamata is stunning in appearance but in its wild habitat, in South America, you will have to be very sharp-eyed to catch even a glimpse of this carnivore, which hunts mainly at night.

In the eastern USA a *Trionyx ferox* tortoise lifts itself out of the water with difficulty. Despite its soft shell this tortoise is aptly named: it will attack anything that moves.

A PERISCOPE SNOUT

Soft-shelled tortoises spend most of their time at the bottom of the water where they scratch through the mud to find their prey. These tortoises, which are more or less deaf and dumb, use their snouts to sniff out their food. To breathe they stick their short snout up out of the water like a periscope. Most of these aquatic species only leave the water to lay their eggs.

A DECOMPOSING SHELL

The matamata is master of disguise with its pustules, inbuilt nooks and crannies and its seaweed-covered humps. It looks like a rubbish heap and can stay motionless for hours – but it can extend its neck to pounce with incredible speed when necessary.

The matamata lies in wait for its prey disguised as aquatic detritus. When a fish passes by its head, which looks like a dead leaf, it is snapped up and swallowed in a few minutes.

Insect-lovers par excellence,
anteaters
are the vacuum cleaners of the jungle

The two-toed anteater is a small anteater the size of a squirrel. The name highlights its difference from other species of anteater, which have three toes. It uses its powerful claws to tear open ant-hills and then feasts on the contents. It is specially adapted to living in the trees and only comes down to ground level when it has to. When it appears the two-toed anteater utters an extraordinary warbling sound.

A PIPE FOR A HEAD

The giant anteater would not look out of place in the cast of *Star Wars* or *The Muppet Show*. It is about the size of a sheepdog, with a long, tube-shaped snout and a tail ending in a hairy, two-tone plume. Yet this is no intergalactic monstrosity: like the armadillo and the sloth it is a member of a very distinct group of mammals – the Edentates. The creature's diet, composed exclusively of ants and termites, was responsible for the evolution of its extraordinary physique: its head, which looks like an extension of its neck, hangs downward like a tube. Its tiny jaws show no trace of teeth but are very useful for capturing insects crawling about underground.

Native Americans have a delightful name for the lesser anteater: they call it *yurumi*, which means 'little mouth' in the Guarani language. The mouth in question is perfectly shaped for catching not only termites and ants but also worms, insect larvae and berries. It does not have teeth, though, and likes its food to come without claws or spines.

The giant anteater may not have any teeth but its stomach contains little stones which help it crush the shells of the insects it devours. The mothers feed their young by regurgitating this highly nourishing insect purée.

In the impenetrable jungles of South America, young giant anteaters have a hard life. Female anteaters give birth standing up, leaving the little ones to climb up on their mother's back by themselves. The baby anteater takes refuge on its mother's back for nearly two years, giving out small, high-pitched squeaks which are the only sign of its presence: it blends in perfectly with its mother's coat.

Lunchtime for the giant anteater. It catches termites with its sticky tongue which whizzes in and out of its elongated muzzle at a rate of 160 times per minute. As a result the animal produces impressive quantities of saliva.

The giant anteater lives exclusively on land and its territory extends from Costa Rica to North Argentina on the South American continent. The jaguar and the puma are its main enemies, which it seeks to escape by fight rather than flight.

Profile

Giant anteater
Myrme-cophaga tridactyla
Family: edentate mammals

Size: 1.3 m
Weight: 35 kg
Habitat: forests and bush savannahs of South America
Diet: ants and termites
Young: weigh only 1700 g at birth
Predators: jaguar, puma
Life expectancy: 15 years in captivity

ANTS FOR EVERY MEAL

The anteater's long sticky tongue acts like a piston, whizzing up and down inside its tubular snout. It can reach into the corridors of the insect colony which the anteater has ripped open with its strong claws and gather up the delicious ants inside.

Dry savannah is the giant anteater's preferred habitat. It does not drink: it absorbs moisture by licking up dew. It has sharp hearing, a fine sense of smell and, surprisingly, is an good swimmer.

The lesser anteater is a small tree-dwelling anteater which the Indians call *caguaré* ('the stinker of the forest'). Like the polecat it gives off a nauseous smell when it is attacked. When the lesser anteater is frightened it stands up on its rear paws and spreads its arms wide like a bear. When it is more seriously alarmed it hisses like a cat.

The praying mantis blends in perfectly with its environment.

Plants or insects?
It's not easy to tell!

PERFECT DISGUISES

In nature, camouflage is crucial. Sometimes the disguise is so successful that it fools even the most vigilant of predators. How could the bird know that underneath that ordinary-looking leaf there is in fact the succulent body of an insect? And it is difficult to spot the head and limbs of an arthropod in what looks like a simple branch or twig. A number of species specialize in imitating foliage in this way: phasmids, leaf insects, grasshoppers and praying mantises all merge perfectly with their green surroundings. Some even take the mimicry a stage further, falling like a dead leaf when they are touched. These fake plants are not even that concerned if you pull off a leg or two: they will simply grow replacements at the next moulting.

Leaf insects are light green in colour during the day. At nightfall they become darker. Another distinguishing feature: most of these insects are parthenogenetic, in other words the females can reproduce unisexually, without the assistance of the male.

This grasshopper is perfectly camouflaged within its plant habitat and safe from its enemies. Unlike leaf insects and praying mantises, this insect's green colouring is due not to chlorophyll absorbed with its food but to a pigment produced by the insect itself. The proof: even when deprived of chlorophyll the grasshopper retains its beautiful emerald green mantle.

The leaf insect is the perfect plagiarist, imitating every aspect of its botanic subject: the colour and the jagged edges, the twisted leafstalk, the minutest of veins. This performance is called 'mimicry'. It even behaves like a leaf: it never jumps, and moves only with the greatest circumspection.

Radar systems and defence mechanisms:
electric fish
have power to spare

Torpedo fish, or electric rays, can deliver an electric shock of up to 200 volts. They are found in all seas up to a depth of 250 metres. Torpedo fish measure nearly 60 centimetres in length and their disk-shaped body has lovely marbling and eye-shaped markings. To hunt their prey torpedo fish camouflage themselves by burrowing into the sand where they patiently lie in wait for their victims.

HOW TO SEE IN THE DARK

Electricity is not just something that is delivered through sockets and wires to run the appliances in our homes. It is all around us: in the air, in the water, in the earth. To create an electric current just rub a plastic ruler over a pullover: this produces static electricity. This level of electric current may be too low for us to observe, but it would not escape the elephant-snout fish. These little fish in tropical Africa live in murky water and are generally active at night. Eyes are no help at all in these gloomy conditions and so these fish have developed their own personal radar system: an organ that is sensitive to the slightest variation in electric current

The electric eel is greatly feared in South America. This 2-metre long eel, which swims just below the surface of the water, can electrocute mammals as big as a cow or a horse. Its charge is the most powerful in the animal kingdom.

Inbuilt power station

The electric organs of the torpedo fish look rather like jelly, but in fact they are muscles which have developed into electricity generators, negative on the lower side and positive on the upper side. The electric field of the torpedo fish consists of 4 to 10 waves which radiate around its body. When hunting, the fish envelops its victim with its fins and finishes it off with an electric shock.

produced by another animal or even by an immobile object. This organ also produces electricity but it is not powerful enough to deliver a shock like that of the fearsome electric eel.

THE ELECTRIC EEL AND THE TORPEDO FISH

This 2-metre long eel is renowned and feared in South America. Its personal electricity generators, arranged in pairs on either side of the spinal cord, can produce an electric charge of 550 volts, in other words nearly a kilowatt – enough to kill a horse! An electric eel can electrocute a frog from a metre away: an effective and original method of fishing which is also practised by the torpedo fish. Electric organs occupy nearly the entire body of the torpedo fish, making it unable to use its fins. Instead of hunting it lies in wait for its prey for hours, hidden in the sand. Careless swimmers who tread on this electric minefield receive a shock of 15 to 80 volts – definitely enough to make their hair stand on end.

The elephant-snout fish is perfectly equipped for its murky world. It can find its way around in more or less total darkness thanks to its electroreceptive organ which picks up the slightest modifications in the electric field around it. This organ is located in the fish's tail. Once the fish has located its prey it pinpoints it with its snout.

On four legs, two legs or no legs at all,
lizards
have some unusual ways of getting about

A LEGENDARY CREATURE

Among reptiles the lizard family is the one with the largest number of species. The course of evolution has produced lizards of all shapes and colours, often very different in appearance from the traditional image of the common wall lizard. If you visit the tropical forests of Mexico or Ecuador, for example, you may be able to spot one of these unusual lizards: the basilisk. The basilisk is named after a legendary monster of antiquity, a grotesque hybrid of cockerel and toad.

WALKING ON WATER

Yet this creature can surely claim Messianic status: not content with running along the ground, it can also walk on water! Like the common collared lizard this basilisk can stand up on two feet and speed along the riverbank. On water moves so rapidly that it does not have the time to sink beneath the surface. At a speed of 12 kilometres an hour its broad, widely spaced feet do not even enter the water.

Profile

Basilisk
Basiliscus basiliscus
Family: Saurians
Size: 80 cm
Weight: 200 g

Habitat: only found from south Mexico to Ecuador
Diet: fruit and small animals
Distinguishing features: a brightly coloured crest on its head; besides its extraordinary ability to walk on water the basilisk is also an excellent swimmer and diver (it also hides at the bottom of the water).

No, this is not an earthworm with feet but a legless lizard. The limbs of the amphisbaenians, or worm lizards, have completely regressed during the course of evolution. For example, some now only have two stumps of forelimbs – and no rear limbs at all.

For the basilisk walking on the water is no miracle but a simple way of getting about. Thanks to its speed and lightness this Central American lizard can run over considerable distances without danger of sinking. Basilisks have been seen crossing a lake 400 metres wide – and then coming back again.

Its bloodshot eyes and vertical pupils give the peaceful gecko a somewhat demonic appearance. And yet to evade its disconcerting gaze all you have to do is stand still: this reptile, which hunts at night, has excellent eyesight which is adapted to a mobile world and can only spot moving objects: as soon as an insect stops moving it disappears from the gecko's view.

The collared lizard extends its legs to avoid burning.

Lizard, snake or fish?

This lizard from the skink family has lost its legs and yet it is not a snake.
Its rather unusual physique is particularly well suited to moving around the desert. Indeed when the skink moves in the sand it looks as though it is swimming.

A FOOTHOLD ON HOT OR SLIPPERY TERRAIN

Spider Man is not the only one who can walk on ceilings or on slippery walls. Geckos are good at doing this too, thanks to adhesive pads or 'lamellas' on their feet. The collared lizard has to endure the furnace of the American deserts and can survive temperatures of 45°C, which would kill most other reptiles. Above this the ground becomes too hot and to avoid contact with the white-hot stones the collared lizard lifts its body by extending its legs.

The gecko's enlarged fingers are covered with lamellas which enable it to stick to all types of surface, however steep the slope. Each lamella has microscopic hooks which can attach themselves to the slightest irregularity on the surface: in effect they are not suckers as was long thought to be the case but more like the climbing hooks used by mountaineers.

Like lost sirens from an ancient world
dugongs
are in danger of extinction

Dugongs are huge marine mammals measuring more than 3 metres in length and weighing nearly 300 kilograms. They are also known as 'sea cows' because of their placid appearance and the shape of their snout.

DISTANT COUSINS OF THE ELEPHANTS

In the clear, shallow waters of the Indian coastline, a silhouette that is almost human in appearance rises up out of the water, looks around and emits a resonant 'p-haa' sound. It may look rather like an overweight siren, but in fact this is a dugong.

Like dolphins and seals, dugongs are mammals which have adapted to the aquatic life. These chubby, slow-moving creatures are distant cousins of the elephants, whose feet have been transformed into fins. Their rear limbs still have fingers and for the first months of their life baby dugongs are covered with hair.

Like all mammals, the mother dugong takes great care of her infant, which is more than a metre long.
The male often stays with them but does not seem to help bring up the little one. Suckling takes place on the surface:
the mother tenderly encircles the young dugong with her fins.

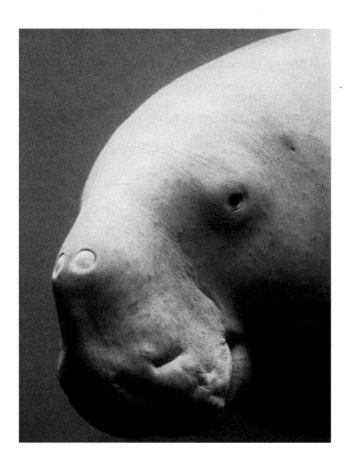

The dugong's eye is adapted to nocturnal vision. Dugongs hunt only at night, and generally in those areas where they themselves are most actively hunted.

The males' incisors stick out, looking strangely like the remnants of elephant tusks. Dugongs belong to the Sirenian order of mammals. These massive creatures gave rise to the Greek legend of sirens, evoked by Homer in the *Odyssey*. In fact on closer inspection the dugong, with its ample covering of fat, hardly lives up to the classical ideal of beauty.

Profile

Dugong
Dugong dugong
Family: Sirenians
Size: 2.5 m to 3 m
Weight: 150 kg
to 200 kg
Habitat: shoreline of the Red Sea, Indian Ocean and Australia
Diet: only 4 types of seaweed of the *Cycomodea* species
Predators: sharks, killer whales and above all humans
Young: the mother cares for them attentively during the first few months
Life expectancy: unknown

A LIVING LEGEND

Christopher Columbus was very disappointed when he spotted dugongs in the Caribbean: 'I observed three sirens,' he wrote,'which were far from being as beautiful as those described by Homer'. In 1560 the doctor of the Viceroy of Portugal made the first scientific observation of dugongs and defined them as 'creatures in every respect comparable to humans'. Even in the 20th century the dugongs have caused some confusion: in 1905 the captain of a cargo ship thought he saw three shipwrecked sailors, but when he headed to rescue them realized he had seen a family of dugongs. Today the it is the dugongs themselves that are in need of being rescued: the species is heading for extinction.

An endangered species

Dugongs like to live in shallow, murky seawater with temperatures of between 20ºC and 36ºC. They are to be found along the shorelines of the Red Sea, the Indian Ocean and less commonly the China Sea. In the 19th century large shoals were a common sight along the north Australian coasts. However, they were systematically hunted for their flesh and now these creatures are timid and difficult to approach.

The dugong has the teeth of a herbivore. To clean the seaweed, which is covered with sand and parasites, the dugong shakes it vigorously, just as elephants do with plants.

Satanic-looking but harmless,
molochs
are perfectly adapted to desert conditions

The moloch is brilliantly adapted to the desert climate. The hump on the nape of its neck contains a fat reserve which it can burn off to provide the water it needs. Another distinguishing feature: as soon as the moloch comes into contact with water all the minute capillary channels in its skin swell and within a few seconds it is fully distended like a balloon. The liquid is channelled directly to the commissures of the lizard's mouth.

THE LITTLE DEVIL OF THE DESERT

Despite its rather off-putting appearance this spiky lizard is completely harmless, except to the ants which constitute its diet.

From head to toe the moloch is covered with scaly spines. The two particularly prominent spines at the top of its skull explain its alternative name of 'thorny devil'. The moloch's colouring is a strange mixture of yellow, red and brown, varying to suit the colour of the earth. Because of its small size (barely 20 centimetres long), its spiky, plant-like appearance and its mimetic colours, the moloch is perfectly camouflaged and can wander around peacefully, safe from predators.

The strange moloch inhabits the deserts and steppes of southern and central Australia, where it lives on a diet of ants, its only food. It has a very mobile tongue which can lick up 20 to 30 insects a minute, or a total of 1800 at each meal! Its molars are very well adapted to crushing insect shells.

The moloch is only found in the deserts of Australia. The Aborigines have many legends about it but have never endangered it in any way. It was the colonials who christened this harmless reptile the 'thorny devil'.

The moloch also uses its hump to scare off predators. When it is attacked the 'thorny devil' places its head between its rear legs, leaving its hump sticking out in front like a sort of second head. This deception can save its life: if an attacker bites off this false head it will be making off with no more than a lump of fat.

With eight legs
octopuses
are never bored!

The octopus can hide in the smallest hole or crevice, springing out on its prey.

A BAD REPUTATION

This exotic-looking creature with its long tentacles armed with suckers and its vigilant eye has always fascinated us. Many have depicted it as a fearful monster. The Greek philosopher Aristotle was convinced that a prawn caught in the same net as an octopus would die of fright! In ancient Greece it was believed that octopuses were able to leave the sea and commit crimes on land.

There may indeed be one or two species in the Indian and Pacific Oceans that are dangerous to humans, but on the whole the octopus is a timid and inactive creature.

Sexual reproduction

Cephalopods have anunconventional method of reproduction. The male has a special 'arm', the hectocotylus, which he inserts into the mantle of the female. This extra limb delivers the spermatophores which fertilize the eggs.

The octopus is a master of camouflage, blending in perfectly with its marine environment. It can even give its body a surface roughness to mimic the rocks in which it lies hidden.

The female octopus lays up to 500,000 eggs, joined in strings, which she hangs from the roof of her shelter. She looks after the garlands for several months, without eating... and then she dies.

EIGHT TENTACLES AND A BEAK

The octopus always has eight legs: no more, no less. If a leg is cut off it will grow back again. Every leg of this marine Vishnu is covered with a double row of suckers which are used to immobilize its prey – generally crustaceans or small fish.

The octopus skilfully directs its prey (still living) towards its mouth and paralyses it with a powerful toxin. Then, using its 'beak' composed of two formidable jaws it can crush the shell of even the toughest crustaceans.

A HIGHLY INTELLIGENT MOLLUSC

The octopus is more than just physically dexterous: it is also something of an intellectual. In fact it belongs to the cephalopod family (the word means 'head and foot'), the most highly evolved of the molluscs. The brain of the octopus is reminiscent of vertebrates' brains in terms of its advanced development and its learning ability. Octopuses have even been known to learn to pull a string to open up a crab trap!

The octopus can change colour radically and instantaneously thanks to its pigmentation cells, called 'chromatophores'. Young octopuses have exactly 70 chromatophores (shown in red in the picture). Over time the number of chromatophores increases and the octopus develops its mimetic powers.

The invertebrate body of the octopus, called its mantle, is surmounted by a pair of globe-shaped eyes. The mantle surrounds a cavity which holds water: this water is expelled violently by the octopus using a funnel that can be pointed in different directions. This current propels the animal in the opposite direction. To escape predators it can also spray a jet of ink which obscures its retreat.

The eyes of the octopus function in much the same way as a camera. The eye has a cornea, an iris, a crystalline lense and a retina: it is as highly evolved as that of vertebrates. The octopus also has a highly developed brain giving it a surprisingly advanced level of intelligence. And yet this underwater intellectual is no more than a mollusc, like the common or garden mussel.

They may not have any fur, but
Mexican hairless cats
are favourites in competitions

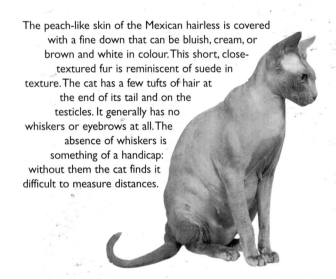

The peach-like skin of the Mexican hairless is covered with a fine down that can be bluish, cream, or brown and white in colour. This short, close-textured fur is reminiscent of suede in texture. The cat has a few tufts of hair at the end of its tail and on the testicles. It generally has no whiskers or eyebrows at all. The absence of whiskers is something of a handicap: without them the cat finds it difficult to measure distances.

THE ET OF THE CAT WORLD

The Mexican hairless is the product of man-made selection, following the birth of a hairless kitten in Canada in 1966 (the absence of hair was due to a genetic disorder). Crossing this kitten with its mother produced more bald kittens which now constitute a new feline breed on their own account. Some people find this wrinkled creature distasteful and even alarming to look at. However it has been accepted in cat shows since the early 1980s. With its long, slender paws and its prominent cheekbones it is the supermodel of the cat world.

The Mexican hairless cat is a man-made creature produced by cross-breeding, and a curiosity that is very popular in cat shows. In terms of appearance this strange cat has been likened to a monkey, a dog, even a baby; in terms of temperament it has all the poise of a top model – it is famed for its patience and it always holds its head high.

The Mexican hairless cat is wrinkled like an old person. Its body temperature is around four degrees higher than that of its fellow felines, making it the perfect companion for those long winter evenings. At first it was thought that its hairlessness might make it the perfect solution for people with a cat allergy. Unfortunately it has a very fine down which gets everywhere.

Sea horses, sea dragons and pipefish

have mastered the art of disguise

CREATURES OF LEGEND

Sea horses have fascinated humans since antiquity and have given rise to a large number of legends. Ground sea-horse mixed with fat was regarded as a cure for baldness. Mixed with wine it was a violent poison and even today in Asia sea-horse eyes fetch high prices for their supposed aphrodisiac qualities. These much-coveted fish with their horse-like appearance look all set to gallop away as you approach them: but in fact they are poor swimmers and have had to develop alternative survival strategies.

CAMOUFLAGE EXPERTS

The sea horse has a single, delicate dorsal fin which enables it to swim vertically or remain stationary: it is not designed for a quick escape. And so it opts for disguise: its body is the perfect shape and colour to pass for a tuft of seaweed, a strategy similar to that of the sea dragon.

Profile

Sea dragon
Phyllopteryx foliatus

Family: Syngathidae

Size: 30 cm long
Habitat: off the south coast of Australia
Diet: small crustaceans
Distinguishing features: strips of skin covering its body in perfect imitation of seaweed

Among this group of marine creatures, the sea dragon is undoubtedly the most gifted at camouflage: the appendages on its back are a perfect imitation of submarine vegetation. As it swims through the water it looks like a piece of floating seaweed. Sea horses live in the kelp fields swept by the tide, attaching themselves to marine plants by their prehensile tail.

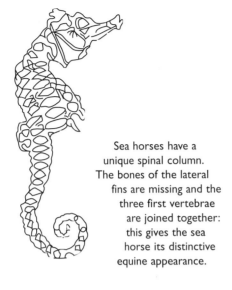

Sea horses have a unique spinal column. The bones of the lateral fins are missing and the three first vertebrae are joined together: this gives the sea horse its distinctive equine appearance.

The Australian sea dragon is a perfect example of camouflage in a coral-reef setting: its strange appearance and its bright colour enable it to pass unnoticed.

As for pipefish, they prefer to mimic plant stems. All day long they remain completely motionless, their body stretched out. For these fish the best form of refuge is provided by the sea cucumber, that bizarre elongated animal which is related to starfish and sea urchins.

SEA-HORSE COMMUNICATION

Sea horses are able to produce sounds in order to communicate. The sounds, which resemble clicking fingers, are probably produced by rubbing the skull bones together. To do this the animal lifts its head as far as possible, as if stretching its neck. The sounds are used both to issue warnings and to attract mates.

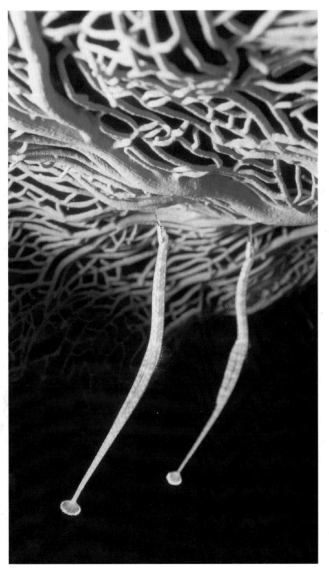

Pipefish are a highly original type of sea creature: their long, straight bodies could easily be mistaken for plant stems.

Geographic distribution

Sea dragons and sea horses are only found along the southern coasts of Australia. Despite their camouflage they are hunted by many predators: skate, small coastal sharks, pacific mackerel, scorpionfish and many other carnivorous fish. However, as for many other animals, the most fearsome predators of all are humans.

MATING RITUALS

Sea horses' mating dance looks something like a delicate eastern dance, executed at a very leisurely pace. This elegant waltz starts with formal preliminaries, bows and salutations between the partners. Once these formalities are dispensed with the sea horse couples dance cheek-to-cheek with their tails intertwined, performing small rhythmic movements. During this embrace the female presses her stomach, bloated with its mature ovaries, against that of the male. The male opens

Males giving birth

Among sea horses it is the male that carries the offspring. Male sea horses have an incubation pouch on their flank. The sides of this pocket form a kind of 'placenta' which provides oxygen and a nutritive liquid for the developing embryos.

his incubation pouch and the female lays her eggs in it (they are fertilized in the process). After this the female has completed her familial duties and the male is left to look after the offspring.

Sea dragons are highly effective mimics. On their head and the rest of their body they have strips of skin which help them blend in with the coral reefs. The head ends in a tubular snout with a tiny, toothless mouth.

Like fairytale dragons,
dracos
glide through the air

Profile

Draco
Draco volans
Family: reptiles
Size: around 20 cm
Weight: less than 300 g
Diet: insects
Habitat: virgin forest of the Indonesian archipelago, rubber or kapok tree plantations
Young: the female lays 1 to 4 eggs in the earth: a very small number for a reptile; however the tropical climate enables these animals to breed all through the year

A LIVING MYTH

This small lizard hidden away in the treetops in the dense tropical forests of South-East Asia blends perfectly with the bark of the trees and could pass entirely unnoticed. Until it launches itself into the sky, that is, unfolding a dazzling pair of wings (orange-yellow and bright blue in colour) and embarking on a gliding flight through the air. This is the draco, or flying lizard. Unlike birds and bats the draco does not have arm-like wings but folds of skin in its sides. They are not really wings at all: the draco does not flap them but uses them to glide on the currents of the air. It spends its life gliding from tree to tree in this way. Visits to ground level are rare: its only reason for coming down to earth is to lay its eggs underground.

The sixteen known species of draco live in the Philippines, Malaysia, the Indonesian archipelago and the south of India. They spend their time basking in the sun to warm their delicate bodies. Males spend a good deal of time folding and unfolding their colourful 'wings'. They do this to ward off enemies and rivals and to pay court to females.

The mating season starts when the draco displays its sparkling colours. It has a fold of bright yellow skin under the chin which it extends as far forward as possible. It also agitates its 'wings' nervously.

The draco's 'wings' are in fact flaps of skin attached to its flanks and generally folded back flat against the body. When it unfolds these wings the draco suddenly takes on a fantasic, mythical appearance. It can glide over a distances of some 10 metres, using its tail to guide it. When it lands it stands upright to brake more effectively, standing delicately on its hind legs like the most elegant of birds.

Creative workshop

*Having studied all of these creatures,
it's time to get creative.*

*All you need are a few odds and ends and a little ingenuity,
and you can incorporate some of the animals we've seen
into beautiful craft objects.*

*These simple projects will give you further insight into the
animal kingdom presented in the pages of this book.*

*An original and simple way to enjoy
the wonderful images of the animal kingdom.*

Sea-horse brooch

Flying fish picture frame

Lizard plant pot

Bat jewellery box

Sea-horse brooch

*I*n the marine depths, the sea horse takes care to camouflage itself; this is your chance to allow it to stand out in daylight, as a brightly coloured brooch.

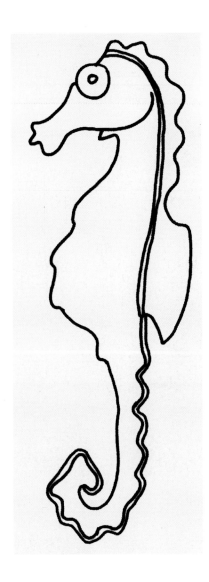

Working on the clay

Trace the design.

On the metal tray, roll out the dark turquoise clay thinly so that it is a little larger than the design.

Place the tracing paper on the rolled-out clay and, with a knife or a needle, mark out the design on to the clay.

Cut around the sea horse shape, setting aside the edges of the clay.

Repeat the same steps with the dorsal fin. The two pieces of coloured clay will join together.

With the orange clay, make a thin strip, rolling it with your fingers, and then sticking it along the back of the sea horse.

Make the eye, and put it in place: a small ball of orange clay on a ball of pale turquoise clay.

Heating

Follow the instructions on the packet for temperature and the time needed to bake the clay.

When the clay has cooled, glue the pin on to the back using a strong glue.

The brooch does not need to be varnished as the modelling clay is brightly coloured.

Leftover clay

You could make two smaller sea horses to wear as earrings, or as beads for a necklace.

You can vary the colours of the design – modelling clay is available in a wide range of shades, including fluorescent and glitter varieties.

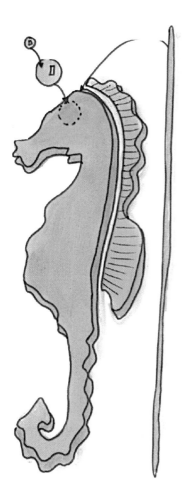

Materials

• Fimo modelling clay in three colours: dark turquoise, pale turquoise and orange • metal attachment to pin brooch on to clothes • tracing paper • sharp knife • oven • metal tray (to work on and to bake the clay)

Flying fish picture frame

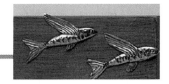

*S*traight from the sea, these flying fish will frame your favourite photographs.

Painting the frame

Paint the frame using blue acrylic paint. Allow this to dry completely, then paint a layer of very diluted white acrylic paint (the consistency of milk). Wipe over it with a sponge to produce a mottled effect, or use a hard brush to create a streaky effect.

The waves

Cut out a piece of brass the same width as the frame, and 10 centimetres longer (to fold over top and bottom).

Trace the design and place the tracing paper over the strip of brass. Draw over the outline with the ballpoint pen (1). Then draw over the line again with an empty ballpoint pen to imprint the design deeper into the metal. Cut around the top edge of the wave design with scissors or a Stanley knife (be careful of the cut metal edges, and small splinters of metal that can be result).

Using neoprene glue, stick the waves on to the bottom of the frame.

Fold the sides of the metal band and glue them around the frame.

The fish

Photocopy the fish designs, increasing or decreasing their size to fit your frame. Lightly trace round the outline of the fish on the right side of the metal sheet.

On the reverse, use a ballpoint pen to firmly mark the lines on the tail and the fins, and mark the small circle of the eye.

Cut around the outlines of the fish. Glue them on to the frame with strong glue.

Finishing
Complete the decoration with a few bubbles, depicted using small blue beads attached with strong clear glue.

Materials

• a wide pale wooden frame • a piece of brass sheeting (available in craft shops) • blue beads • two tubes of acrylic paint in blue and white • a sheet of tracing paper • a tube of neoprene glue • a small sponge • a ballpoint pen • scissors or a Stanley knife

Lizard plant pot

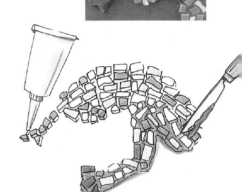

*D*ecorate an old plant pot with this attractive ceramic lizard.

Preparation

Pot: trace the outline of a lizard freehand on to the pot using a soft lead pencil. When you are happy with the design, draw it on with felt-tip.

Mosaic: using the tile cutter, cut the yellow and dark brown tiles into smaller pieces (rectangles, squares and triangles).

IMPORTANT: it is essential to wear protective glasses for this stage, and it is advisable to cut the tiles in a transparent plastic bag to avoid the pieces flying in all directions.

Making the mosaic

Glue the yellow and brown ceramic pieces within the shape of the lizard, varying the colours to give the effect of scales.

Leave a small space between the tiles for the grouting.

To make the lizard's feet, use brown pieces of tile, cut in long sections.

Take two green tiles from the mixed sachet and cut them into diamond shapes to make the eyes, and use red tiles for the tongue.

Then glue maroon, grey and blue tiles to the pot to make the background.

Diamond pattern: around the top of the pot, glue a row of pale grey tiles, then a row of dark brown tiles.

Wait at least 24 hours for the glue to dry before applying the grouting.

Applying the grouting

Clean the pot and erase all traces of the pencil line.

Prepare the grouting, following the manufacturer's instructions.

Using a palette knife, spread the grouting over the mosaic, filling the spaces between the tiles. This stage of the process needs to be done with care, because it is this that gives the 'finish' to the mosaic.

When the grouting starts to take, clean off any excess from the tiles with a damp sponge.

Leave to dry for an hour, then polish the tiles with a dry cloth.

Finish

For an attractive patinated finish, put a layer of clear wax on the terracotta pot and use brown shoe-polish to highlight the streaks on the pot.

Materials

• terracotta flower pot (at least 20 centimetres in diameter)
• a small tile cutter • a tube of ceramic glue • a pot of brown grouting • small ceramic tiles in the following colours: golden yellow (2 sachets), dark brown (1 sachet), pale grey (1 sachet), maroon (1 sachet), and mixed colours (1 sachet) • a soft lead pencil • a felt-tip pen • a palette knife • a sponge • plastic protective glasses

Bat jewellery box

*T*his bat looks as though it has flown straight from a haunted castle, to decorate a Halloween-style box.

Preparing the box

Prepare the plaster of Paris: one measure of water to two measures of powder (leftover mixture will keep for a few weeks in a sealed container in the fridge).

Leave the paste for 30 minutes. Then spread it on to all visible sides of the box, using a palette knife. This gives a slightly uneven surface.

Leave to dry for 24 hours.

During this time, trace the shape of the bat on to the cartridge paper. Cut it out. Spread small pieces of string with vinyl glue and glue them on to the wings and feet of the bat. Using a little plaster of Paris, form the body and the head. Leave to dry for 24 hours.

Decorating the box

Glue pieces of string on to the sides of the box.

Paint the whole box with dark blue paint, highlighting it with mid-blue paint.

Paint the bat in turquoise.

Once the paint is dry, glue the mirror and the bat on to the lid with solvent-free glue (to avoid damaging the mirror). Leave to dry for at least one hour.

Make a frame for the mirror by glueing two pieces of string round it and using plaster of Paris to build it up. Leave to dry for at least 24 hours.

Paint the frame of the mirror with pale yellow paint.

Enhance all the edges of the box using a palette knife dipped in dark gold paint. Then give a patina effect using a very diluted solution of dark brown acrylic paint.

Use false gems to make the bat's eyes, and to decorate the box.

Materials

• a wooden box (the box shown is 19 centimetres long, by 12.5 centimetres wide, by 6 centimetres high) • a packet of plaster of Paris powder • a tube of solvent-free multi-use glue (for use on the mirror) • a pot of vinyl glue (wood glue) • a small round mirror (8 centimetres in diameter) • string and a small piece of cartridge paper • small false gems • acrylic paint in mid-blue, dark blue, turquoise, pale yellow, dark gold and dark brown • a palette knife • a paintbrush

Photographic credits

Colibri: J.M. Brunet: 44b; P. Etcheverry: 48b; D. Fontaine: 44a; AM. Loubsens: 42b; J.H. Maraindaz: 48a; J.L. Paumard: 15a, 13, 49

Jacana: Jean-Louis Dubois: 60a

Nature: Bassot: 25b; Bassot/H. Chaumeton: 20-21, 22a, 23, 24, 25a, 25c; Bignon: 38a; H. Chaumeton: 12-13, 16b, 22b, 22c, 58b, 59, 70a, 72, 73; H. Chaumeton/Lanceau: 19a, 39, 52a, 52b, 53b, 53c, 70b, 70c; Ferrero: 6a, 6b, 8, 10a, 11a, 26a, 26b, 68a, 68b, 69; Gohier: 18a, 18b, 19b, 36c, 37a, 54b, 55a, 57; Grospas: 15b, 53a; Lanceau: 11b, 36b, 38b, 42a, 45, 56b; Dr. Frieder Sauer: 14b, 16a, 28, 29, 37b, 60b, 71

Okapia: Jean-Loup Blanchet: 58b; Fred Bruemmer: 16c; Joe Mc Donald: 17, 62-63; Jett Foott: 36a; Andreas Hartl: 34-35; Armin Maywald: 47; Mark Newman: 58a (1988); Dr. Eckart Pott: 33a; Alan Root: 7, 9, 10b, 30b, 54a, 55b; Tui de Roy: 32b; Dr. Frieder Sauer: 65b; Konrad Wothe: 43

Phone: Didier Brandelet: 41, 78a; Ben Croop/Auscape: 66b; J.P. Ferrero: 27, 46, 50-51, 51, 80, 81a, 81b; J.P. Ferrero/J.M. Labat: 30a, 31; François Gohier: 56a, 65a; Ian Gordon/Auscape: 33b; Mark Jones/Auscape: 32a; Jean-Michel Labat: 61, 74a, 74b, 75; Labat/Jardel: 14a, 64; J.M Labat/Lanceau: 40; Parer & Parer-cook/Auscape: 66a, 67a, 67b; Becca Saunders/Auscape: 76-77, 78b (International SND), 79

Acknowledgements

The publishers would like to thank all those who have contributed to this book, in particular:
Evelyne Alice Bridier, Antoine Caron, Michèle Forest, Anne Jochon, Nicolas Lemaire,
Hervé Levano, Kha Luan Pham, Vincent Pompougnac,
Marie-Laure Sers-Besson, Emmanuelle Zumstein

Illustration: Franz Rey
Translation: Sue Rose and Susan Mackervoy for Ros Schwartz Translations - London, Sarah Snake

Printing: Eurolitho - Milan
Dépôt légal September 1998
Printed in Italy